D

Dear Son,

Tyree, thank you! None of any of it could ever be possible without you. I am forever grateful that God gifted you to me. I love you and I'm very proud of you. Love, Mom

To My Family,

Dear Mom, LaShanna, Tony, Audrey, Auntie Pam, Uncle Greg and Alicia, thank you for being my village. I love you.

Dear Grandpa Felton,

I think of you often, and I feel you with me. Thank you for never giving up on me. It's your voice inside my head that tells me I can do whatever I put my mind to. I love you and I'll see you on the other side some day.
Love, Tawana

Dear Ancestors,

You are so many. You've carried me so far. Thank you for the journeys traveled and those yet to come.

Ivoire, Please keep that pen moving! Your poems are life changing. Love, Honeycomb

love - ust

You peeled back the layers of my resistance, fractured my ego on concrete walls stacked up to fence me from your charm. I needed to trust your harm was unintentional, that the daggers you threw once belonged to cupid and the stupid things we did were consequences of fragility, our immaturity. Young lovers misguided, hiding behind masks of insecurity. We lusted ourselves into frustration, sulking into our lower vibrations, lost inhibitions.
I wonder if you knew this. You used to be the one that got away.
A different time, a different day, I just might tell you to your face.

Black City

My city got a black eye
for loving Black people.
Global Black metropolis
written off as evil.

They starved us of resources,
but the D is persistent.
We keep standing up,
Detroit is resistance.

They want us ashamed,
want us running for cover,
want us turning our backs,
while they pushing us under.

Got the same politician
who poisoned Flint city
talking bout give him some time,
he promise to fix it.

Walking around free
while people still dying.
If you turn on the TV
you can catch his ass lying.

Controlling the city
like his personal bank.
Meanwhile gentrifiers flock
like we ain't on the slate.

The D is a mecca.
So don't get it twisted.
We be churning em out.
Young, Black and Gifted

{R}evolutionary Big Sister

revolutionary big sister
I miss you
the way you waged love in the struggle
kicked butt
and took names in the crisis
the way you called evil out
and pulled young folks in was a science
your defiance was strategic
and you teased me
for carrying a notebook to study your moves
but, I never met anyone like you
you were like a walking computer,
A heart with no limitations
your vision was contagious
from Africa to Palestine
folks picked up your rallying cry
Wage Love in this water fight, you said
your body is gone, but your spirit ain't dead
and we keep on moving
pursuing our humanity
resisting this insanity
from outside forces
they want us to breakdown
give up and turn on each other
but you left us instructions
so we'll keep on with your guidance
you told us water is life
so we'll keep on trying
to humanize one another
Waging love in this struggle
for generations to come
or at least until the revolution
for our humanity is won

(Dedicated to Ancestor Charity Hicks)

Revolutionary Brother

you are not the man you used to be
a mere fragment of your destiny
you traversed the same concrete
you used to lug across your back
they wrote you off as irredeemable
a leech
a blood sucker on society
and you believed their condemnation
buried your dignity deep inside their plantation
like many Black boys have done before you
you were young with no direction
lost inside the oxymoron of corrections
you entered that place a broken soul
unprepared to take your role inside humanity
so they wrote you off
another melanated brother doomed to rot inside their cell
you gave your family hell
but they fought for you
sought your redemption
in a system rigged for you to fail
I guess they didn't know you well
cause you gained your manhood in that wreck
recaptured your dignity
lost in adolescence
God gave you a calling and you answered
removed the bastard from your psyche
rebuilt the home you once destroyed
misguided boy
chiseled into a revolutionary
the world has witnessed your elevation through storms
trials and tribulations
you stood firm in your conviction
and it was your redemption
that brought you here

A Poem for Charity

I listened for your voice in the waves, but couldn't find it.
cause they privatized it, the land around our water.
Dear Daughter Warrior of the Nations, you were courageous.

You elevated us into the struggle.
Your spirit was untouchable,
unlike the land they keep grabbing,
attacking our humanity.

But I find sanity in the trees,
in the comrades who won't lay down without a fight.
Water is a human right you said.
They may have killed you dead, but we're still here,
carrying the torch you left behind!

They cannot dampen our spirits any longer.
Though they keep attacking our resources,
our land and our water.
We do not thirst in vain, cause we are survivors,
providers of each others needs.

We bleed truth into our conditions,
stand firm in our conviction.
We'll get through this genocidal expedition,
waging love along the way.
So, I dedicate this poem to you today.
And I say, thank you Dear Charity,
for providing the clarity we all needed.

You gave your life so that we may live simply,
with empathy, compassion and humility.
And for you, we'll do just that,
while we fight to reclaim our dignity back!

Tangela

Tangela, you were a fearless servant,
deserving of your Ancestral recognition
a movement voice against oppression.

You put on for your people daily,
sacrificed your health and safety.

You were a warrior,
always dressed to the nines.

A divine spirit,
forcing accountability from the system.

You never let them off the hook,
you kept them shook,
with your brilliant street reporting,
and your boots on the ground authority.

You were a force to be reckoned with.

Tangela you were courageous,
a caregiver, a mother,
a lover of Black people,
humble and powerful.

You made your challenges your strength,
you were a Queen, royal in your spirit,
loyal in your deeds.

You will be missed.

And I would be remiss,
if I didn't thank you for your heart,
it strengthened mine.

You never turned your nose up at anyone.

You were a healer, a listener and a truth teller.

You made the world a better place,
so full of Charity and Grace.

So I give gratitude today,
for all the ways you showed the world how to love.

The 80s

tip toed over needles
in my hood
growing up
drug afflicted
streets riddled
with addiction
neighborhood consequences
too dire for young comprehension
I remember inspecting the corners
before I could step over
to play
plastic tubes
fallen bodies
now we fetishize zombies
I recall living among them
immunized from reality
and family
the 80s was a scary time
one the mind never escapes
I tried
pulled up my She-Ra underoos
and struggled to fly
I still have the scar on my knee
thought I could leap free
from the drama
the saga of my zip code
the stench of the bodies dying around me
Kimberly, Tameka the man nailed to the floor
I wish the horror of my past
was science fiction
that I didn't lose count of the deaths
by adolescence

that I didn't know
so many little girls who'd been molested
the 80s was a scary time
one the mind never escapes
I tried
put on my Wonder Woman cape
and struggled to hide
had no invisible plane to shelter me
now my dreams
play out in sequence
a menace to my maturity
they take me back to younger days
the years my mind would run away
like the day my father died of AIDS
9 years old and clairvoyant
I saw it coming
he denied it
my grief later defined me
the 80s was a scary time
one the mind never escapes
I tried
but memories
are finicky that way

Nature Love

Kiss me against the bark beneath the tree,
but don't forget the leaves long to breathe
your love too.

My Notebook

last night
I left my notebook
in a far away place
stumbled from my bed
discombobulated
out of place
wondering
is it possible to retrace my thoughts
and maintain my sanity
when a book holds the key
to my creativity?

Love Wager

she wakes to the world waging love,
but rarely feels the world reciprocate.
her arrogance is spoon-feeding her,
nudging her to learn
that the journey to grow other's souls
may be righteous
and the deeds may be many
but it is often the soul of the love wager
that the love wager neglects

Revolutionary Poets

revolutionary poets
peel poems
off the scabs
of our existence
clench them tightly
between gums
worn out from resistance
we barely exist
through the pain
in our stories
yet embody
the wisdom
of Ancestors
before us

Capitalism is Hell

blood
sweat
tears

we labor intensively
glorifying our excretion
as if dehydration
and forced anemia
are cause for celebration

we work our fingers to the bone
barely affording the gristle
ass kissing our bosses
as if they shit out mistle
tip toeing around their narcissism

fuck capitalism
the fear it creates
the system it fosters
the write-ups for being late
the CEOs licking their plates
while their employees flounder
the greedy scoundrels
that don't deserve our dollars

it's a difficult thing to shift your frame
but the definition of insanity
is doing the same . . .

Fuck That

I am asked to police my tongue
sufferers don't have the right to speak violently
curse words are the antithesis of silence
they hide behind angry soliloquy
so, I'm told
but fuck that

I'm getting too old to tip toe around oppression
to stay reticent
while babies are poisoned in Flint
and dehydrated in my city

they say they have pity on us
but I pity the souls who stay quiet
while innocence is dying
while government defiantly misrepresents us

so if curse words raise your pressure
and all you can offer is conjecture
then I ask that you reevaluate your priorities
learn the stories of the people who are suffering
and reserve your judgment
for the ones who deserve it

Flight

her wings have been clipped
so she cannot fly
she waddles feverishly
gazing at the sky
fearful of her lower ground
surroundings
it's lonely down here
lingering at the feet of the unknown
she remembers when she used to float away
escape from the kicks and the screams
used to leap safely into the trees
she was less vulnerable
when she had both her wings
she felt beautiful
admired by the two legged species
she never longed to be counted among them
to her, they seemed oblivious
stepping over one another in mundane pursuit
she used to have an aerial view
of their destruction
now she was among them
maneuvering for survival
rivaling among the heels of the tramplers
keenly aware of her futile existence
life was never like this
there was peace among the clouds
there was truth among the hoverers
she spots a fruit
hanging low enough to conquer
takes it into her battered wings
nibbles it with her worn out beak
she realizes she'll breathe another day
scrapping among the stragglers
wondering aimlessly through the breeze
struggling just to be

Survival Ain't Enough

it is not enough to just survive
when the scars of our Ancestors
are invisibilized
and the pride we once held
is buried in strife

it is not enough to just survive
when the cries of our children
go ignored
and the elders are pleading
"study war no more!"

it is not enough to just survive
when the women are forced
to run and hide
from insecure fists
blackening eyes

it is not enough to just survive
when families suffer
cause the well ran dry
the furnace is off
got no light inside

it is not enough to just survive
when Black folks are being trapped
in a system designed
to break us down
and keep us confined

survival may be a key element
but it's not a quick fix
and it's not the end

When Will it End?

We live in times where education must be intervention
must free our children from indoctrination into a system that abuses them, confuses
and misuses them.

We live in times where parents and teachers must be brave,
unhinge the chains of American repression.

We've let our babies internalize false lessons of prosperity,
hypocrisy within the system.

We send them into tunnels with little probability of light,
then fight them when they seek it elsewhere.

When will we tell them the American dream ain't fair,
that it's a nightmare waiting to rip them alive, stomp on their pride and pit them
against their friends for the perception of success?

When will we tell them that the barrel can only hold 1% of the crabs?
That not even the strongest will always survive?

When will we quit lying, quit forcing our children to take pride in debt, fetish over
the things they can't get, even if they try hard?

When will we warn them that the bootstraps are broken, stop pushing them to lift
themselves up on a prayer that's rarely answered?

Your baby is an artist,
he draws all over his paper,
you punish his behavior . . .
he never draws again, his spirit dies within . . .

When will it end?

Oxygen

i gazed at the trees
on the ride home tonight
listened for their limbs
withering in the wind

they whispered welcome in my ear
offered joy for my intrigue
said my affection was refreshing
a blessing from the nature Gods

they told me they had felt abandoned
been reduced to parking spot reminders
and indecency concealers

they remembered how little boys
would swing from them
how little girls would sing to them
they wondered if I still found them beautiful
if I could ever drop by just to talk

i promised to honor their existence
to join in on their resistance
they said they longed for my persistence

i blew them kisses
then walked inside

told them
they don't have to wait for love
til i'm outside

Black Mother . . .

I'm supposed to be a statistic
a product of this wicked system of shame and blame

the kind that don't recognize your name
unless you are dead, "educated" or famous

they want me to be nameless

struggling for spaces of visibility
in a society based on credentials and credibility

they seek out my academic portfolio
cause street cred don't mean much no more
without a grant, some buzz words and victims

I can't be with them
unless they are saving me
I am at risk
a single mother
threatening the paternal order of Black families
accused of gambling with the life of my seed

they blame me for his father's condition
regurgitating Willie Lynch's fictional existence

and honestly it pisses me off
cause I didn't create this

as a matter of fact I hate this
being boxed into perpetual failure

caged by judgmental hypocrisy

they keep trying to sell me this American dream fuckery
and I'm over it

sick of being buried beneath it
so I'm rebuilding anew

with thick skin
loving Black men
but none before myself

I am wealth
spiritually and otherwise connected

my Ancestors are present
and I am healing
revealing my true identity
unapologetically

LOVE

Love
the potion from which my spirit drinks
he is a teen
just over 19
with melanated swag
and though daggers haven't punctured his psyche
he is prey like them all
young Black bodies
with yellow tape on the ready
I tell him if they stop you
hold your head steady
don't twitch
never resist
unball your fists
don't poke out your lips
look straight
wait
look down
this shit is frustrating
cause I don't have the formula
to keep my baby alive
he is pushing six five
and likes hoodies and skittles and tea
and sometimes he sags his jeans
exposing his briefs
it's a fad they treat like a death sentence
and I don't get it
teenagers are supposed to be invincible
we ain't supposed to bury them
I keep praying for some kind of reprieve from this nightmare
sick of having to affirm the value in Black Lives
in a country always appraising us
enslaving us
building trillion dollar industries on our labor
yet they question our behavior

deem us rebellious
thugs in need of saviors
it angers me
that we can't seem to break from this manipulation
and I ain't blaming us
just need us to start waging love
from uniforms to sweats
three piece suits to dresses
cause somewhere we've lost our humanity
and it's time we got it back
before another drop of blood penetrates the pavement

My city

My city got me lodged between paradigms
do I chase a dime? or fight crime?
I can't evade the revolution
I'm neck deep in it
find myself wishin I was sleep again
a sheep again
cause shit getting too hard to swallow
we waterless
got a gov't lawless and unaccountable
taxing us out of our domiciles
but, they blaming us though
say Black people be lazy
only built this country
so why they complaining
poutin bout reparations when they still ain't free
melanated bodies rot in penitentiaries
I never lived in a democracy
we a institutional hypocrisy
dirty in war
raping and torturing poor
innocent blood on the flag
it's the anthem
they sanction lies from the capitol

Free Yo Mind

restore order to your psyche
shake loose the noose from your existence
you're gifted
psychologically encrypted with Ancestral DNA
you stand on shoulder blades
royalty made
can't nobody make you a slave
if your mind is free

Birds . . .

fractured wings
broken beaks
deceased
we keep riding
sleepless nights
for the birds who fall victim to tires
devoured in city streets
unworthy commodities
they perish without reason
pigeons
finches
roadkill
buried in potholes
another human made disaster
normalized
listen for their cries
before they disappear from the sky

Affirm Her

affirm her as is or leave her be
alone does not equate to desperation
when patience is in her virtuous state she is unbothered
inguinally unperturbed
desire shall not secure a space in time
spent with frivolity
she knows joy beyond her loins
and love beyond her heartache
she is wisdom
beyond her years
joyous beyond her tears
revolutionary despite her fears
and whole again
a catch again
yet falling for few
balance is the equalizer
she sought feverishly and captured
so let he who casted his stones the last time
aim again

Make Me Over

make me over
in ignorance and blissful ways
in vertical slumber
make me under
standing idly by
consumed with my own reflection
resurrect my naivety and vanity
recreate the masks I dawned securing the scars on my interior
revive my inferiority complex and lack of understanding
make me apologetic for my resistance to mediocrity
and self-hatred
consume me with lower vibrations
deconstruct my wisdom of the nations and feed me poison
negate all inhibitions
and maximize the frivolity in my choices
I want you to dismantle my self-esteem
and penetrate my psyche
with greed and idolatry
I want to be individualistic
and complicit in my conditions
make me a coconspirator to my devise
and illusive frame of reference
I just don't want to get it
said no one ever

Gullibility

gullibility digs too deep a trench for me
I can hear the souls of my Ancestors
dangling from the trees folks keep pushin me to climb
they say don't mind the sacrifice
the loved ones I'd leave behind
lead them to their boot straps
teach them how to tug em
wrap em snug between their fingers
you can't afford to linger
go count your dimes and claim your freedom
we all got choices
voices
all they gotta do is vote and click their heels
and somehow racism won't be real
and redlining
and genocide
police brutality
and fratricide
but I can't live no fairytale
while our babies are being prepped for cells
glued to boxes
force feeding trauma to their psyches
they trying to sike me
but I won't conceal the pride I feel
in my locks thick lips, hips and melanin
won't turn my back
on my people's plight
to free the land from the oppressors hands
so ignorance will have to wait
lay dormant in its current state
cause I can't be blissful in this shit
til all my people free to live

Single Woman

alone is supposed to mean lonely
38
single
plus she got a cat
no man to round off the equation
she probably crazy
why else she waiting?
age don't recess unless scripted or stitched in
self-esteem don't carry clout no more
you can't be no Black woman self preserving
clairvoyant in your deserving
of a yoke equivalent in spirit
endearing
ancestrally connected
a man done chasing adolescence
a man who sees beauty
as an equal worth protection
more than an erection
kindred in reflection
a beacon of light
a knight who comes home at night
not worried bout no shine
won't shortchange you into a dime
ain't bought into that paradigm of marriage
an urgency for women, a trap set for men
he is accountable honorable, honest, yet imperfect
worthy of monogamy
ready to lead at God's command
a noble man who understands
I'm that part of him
he's yet to find
yet neither of us is lost

Black Mothers

Black Mothers
remember you are warriors
the root of African Nations
courageous, resilient, resolute
you hold truth on your side
you are light in the devastation
makers of ways when there are none
your existence is revolutionary
their institutions
will try and convince you
to chew up and spit out your Black seeds
but you must remain firm
resistant to their racism and heteropatriarchy
they will try
and manipulate your psyche into their bidding
they will lynch you
in the media
champion you
in the media
coerce you
with their thug shaming agenda
but you must be wiser than their tricks
their stones and their sticks
though their words may hurt you will persevere
you are survivors
diamonds polished through flame
you are the calm in torrential rain
the line in the sand is before you
cross over it with village in tow
carry forward the torch of our Ancestors
lift up your vibrations and seek out the answers
you will find they are inside you

Real Talk (abecedarian poem)

Anger, the only right we've got left
Bound by governmental agencies of oppression
Corruption
Dragging poor folks through the mud screaming
Emergency!
Finances need managing, while
Greedy mofos still pocket dough
Hastening the annihilation of Black folks
I wonder how many urban cities got targets
Just minutes away from dictatorship
Keeping the money divided amongst the 1%
Liars, lobbying for more corporate rule
Monopolizing on middle class illusions of grander
No nigga left behind
Opportunists
Promising clean neighborhoods and streetlights
Quenching the thirst of the American Dreamers
Reality done hit my City again
Struck us clean below the waste
Tyrannical rule
Undermines our humanity
Vasectomizing our voices
Where the hell is our democracy?
Xenocracy at its finest!
Yellow bellied
Zabernism may be in action, but they need to deal with the fact that, we ain't leavin!

Life Skills

fresh from the cocoon
ain't even got my colors set
still wet behind the ears
ain't figured how to fly yet

feeling remnants of slime
got caught up in my shell
he said he had my back
but when I leaned on him, I fell

now I could wallow in the pity
drown my pillow in my tears
but I'mma step out on limb
been handling grown-up shit for years

call it a temporary set back
or maybe a hiatus
moved my shit from dramaville
better yet, from the equation

got my focus off of one
and placed priority on me
cleared my head of all the bull
restoration of integrity

True Story

I'm a grassroots educator
you can call me place-based
got no time for naysayers
the movement ain't no race

My people dying waterless
they been thirstin for days
we water warriors in motion
but we ain't lookin for praise

When the media ignored us
some walked for 70 miles
passed out, but didn't stop
some even headed to trial

Most won't remember our journey
when the smoke has cleared
but "we gone be alright"
cause we been down for years

wage {r}EVOLution

Some people say a lot of shit
and do a lot of different shit
I don't profess to be perfection
but, I do know I'm consistent

I worry less about the likes
I get my street cred from my deeds
I'm not set trippin on no hood
my work ain't limited to streets

They say we hopeless in the D
Black and Brown ain't worth the dough
but if that's what's really real
then why they flockin here in droves?

They tore us down in propaganda
we soaked that shit up in our psyche
then turned the hatred on ourselves
now we scrappin over Nikes

Let's put our egos on hiatus
turn our noses down for once
put your fist up in the air
real revolution wages love

water WARriors

I hale from a city
where the water is off
45 from Flinstones
where they picking us off

100K still poisoned
yet Flint's not trending
politicians acting pissed
it's political pretending

calling for the resignation
Of a criminal mind
10 already dead
but he ain't serving no time

28 years under
for the hip hop mayor
racism is evident
but they don't care

activists facing charges
for defending our lives
felonies for water towers
plus the homrich 9

my city dying of thirst
but sit on 20%
they stealing water from us
but we purchasing it

this is the story
of the water wars
it ain't your fault
but the battle is yours

No Deficit

Not functioning from no deficit
I'm heaven sent
Ancestrally guided
3rd eye equipped
I'm relevant
Legitimate
Ebonics sometimes
Still literate
My word is bond
No hypocrite
My glow is contagious
Stop fearin it
I'm wide awake
Not ignorant
If you preachin to choirs
Who hearin it?

Real Love

when you factor in your value
you won't struggle with your worth
you'll lift your head in high regard
put your care and safety first
it's not a selfish thing to self-preserve
in fact, it's necessary
but don't listen to the world
it teaches the contrary

Black Child

Black child
born to Black child
they say
you got no place in this world
fixed of judgments
tell you
yo mama outta be ashamed
for birthing a disaster
a bastard child
raised by adolescents
tell you
you won't get very far
kids like you never do
say you were
doomed at conception
ain't no village to protect you
groom your momma
through her folly
they'll box you deep into a corner
try and condemn your whole existence
tell you
she shoulda made better decisions
used protection
married your father
before you were born
Black child
born to Black child
they will drag you through the mud
but stay resilient
carve your mark into the wind
turn your nose up at the naysayers
and leave the world
better than you entered it

If I Perish Writing Poetry

if I perish writing poetry
i'll rebirth as elegy
scribe haiku between the clouds
testify soliloquy
spit rhyme in abecedarian
breathe creation allegorically
I will prose before the sunrise
and sonnet nocturnally

Village

the apple fell far from the tree
so the village picked up her seed
and replanted him

Don't Sweat Me Then

some folk won't sweat you
less you naked
a little cleavage and some thigh
you can't be no mighty woman
in big britches
and a {r}evolutionary tee
nothing to see here
that shit so 1963
won't give no glimpse
to feed the cyberspace erections
guess she be trippin
like she perfection
or got foresight
a 3rd eye trifecta
her self-esteem
is larger than her backside
and she won't backslide
into pitiful relationships
based on lust
no trust
just thrusts
void of mental ecstasy
her body longing to be free
she got her limbs on reservation
can't let them loose
for speculation is an ally of rumors
derogatory humor
and side talk
so, she'll wait reserved
and free from doubt
and let the Ancestors
point him out

Ego

we carry boulders on our shoulders
when we fail to tune in
skip the mole hill for the mountain
cause we playin to win
but when ego is the strategy
and the team is secondary
the mind becomes the coal mine
the individual the canary

privilege

there's a lot of privilege
that comes from existing
in a world where the structures
line up for your bidding
where the gateway to a city
opens up at your arrival
while it's booting out inhabitants
struggling for survival

there's a lot of privilege
in turning the other cheek
in picking and choosing
the harms that you see
in moving in homes
of the recently displaced
made empty by class
most prominently by race

there's a lot of privilege
in remaining silent
while the city you inhabit
is being dehydrated
while the structures are crumbling
and the schools are attacked
while most of the assaulted
are Brown and Black

there's a lot of privilege
in taking in grants
for communities you just got to
where neighbors who are Black
have been denied resources
are losing their homes
their farms are being mowed down
they're suffering alone

there's a lot of privilege
but it won't grow your soul
the perks of white supremacy
will never make someone whole
only through co-liberation
can we realize the dream
of destroying a system
that thrives
on being inhumane

Purple Legend

you were brave
a haven of creativity

bold
an ego rooted in humility

you held art to epic standard
demanded your respect
you were courageous
outrageous most times

you defined artistic ingenuity
carved out a road
when others picked a lane

your royalty was self proclaimed
and backed up with a vengeance

you stayed consistent
brought the metal to its knees
you were a genius on the keys
a magician on the strings

you channeled doves
when you would sing
i watched in awe
with all the world
even as a little girl

i was a witness to your magic
and losing you is tragic

thank you for your music
Purple Legend

3rd Eye Connect

3 hour nap
but I'm still tired
gotta break out the pen
before I retire

got words on my tongue
dying to leap
got a pad on my pillow
itchin to speak

i'm always hesitant
to pen my late night vibes
don't think bout regular shit
even on Saturday night

i stay plottin and prosin
on the crux of my vision
always shedding off layers
to my mental conditionin

it ain't a popular thing
to be a 3rd eye connect
but my Ancestors got me
so I'm rollin with it

Art Heroes

stop telling us our heroes can't be artists
you are the inspiration for our canvasses
our melodies
we don't just dream for you
we sing for you
and string for you
we sonnet you
and read to you
we dance for you
and paint for you
reveal in art
our pain to you
art takes on the wounds
of our mistakes
regurgitates our hurt
in ways only creative souls
could fathom
art is the umbrella through our storms
the thing that makes our crazy normal
it's in everything we see
art is everything we do
it's in all the things we hear
art is the comfort for our fears
and the shoulder for our tears
some artists leave us with their soul
and it's the art they leave behind
that keeps us whole

Art Legacy

when some artists die
we gain allies
we didn't have
when we were alive

the very art that was resented
will be revered
folks will reminisce over our lyrics
some genuinely
others opportunistic

idiosyncrasies will be forgiven
memories will birth from fiction

we'll be uplifted for our skill
recalled for our good will
quoted for our honesty
our integrity
and celebrity

we'll be deemed conspiracists in our living days

and though we carried sound waves
of political thought
fought the establishment
with our words

those are rarely the verbs
they'll remember us for

The Raccoon Won

a raccoon challenged me to a stare down once
and won
i remember i couldn't run
paralyzed with fear
now i know
what a dear in headlights must feel
i didn't see her coming
oblivious
minding my own business
head tilted to the ground
she crept up on me
didn't make a sound
i screamed and called for backup
my girl ran out and backed me up
from a distance
she wasn't feeling it either
we kept our eye on her
she stared us down
then leaped the fence
i ran for it

Activist Assembly Line

they will martyr you in death
but stretch you thin while you're alive

drag your limbs through near contusion
clock you on the activist assembly line

they'll place your value on their sightings
try and marginalize your work

but you can't focus on the naysayers
you gotta focus on the work

Dr. King was near abandoned
towards the ending of his life

Malcolm X assassinated
while preaching Afro-Americans Unite

it's a serious commitment
when we live in movement times

don't give no energy to bullshit
when your life is on the line

Writers Don't Get Blocked

sometimes
I rip rhymes from my spine
when I'm tryin to rhyme
cut my teeth on my pen
when I'm tryin to write

the words get all jumbled
when I'm tryin to impress
I get caught up in the cadence
and forget the message

there ain't a damn thing
as writers block
ego and insecurity
be putting words on lock

I freed myself from the capture
of the poet boogy man

now the words free flow
from the tip of my pen

Rain

the rain keeps whistling
i listen closely for her
she tells me, stay dry

Don't Make America Great Again

I got a fever for the flavor of liberation
a quenching for the thirst of vindication
a country built on slavery must pay reparations
or at the very least
stop their racial propagation

Black bodies still suffer from redlining
and segregation
then get displaced from safe havens
by gentrification
they poison our water
and attack our education
shut down our schools
then call us uneducated

"it is our duty to fight for our freedom"
"I believe that we will win"
but we must resist the racism
calling us to "make America great again"

Detroit: The City We Won't Let Die

they try and erase us
rename us
displace us
but we ain't faceless
our bodies are here
BOLD, BLACK, BEAUTIFUL
we shed tears from the sweat
of our Ancestors
bask in the glory of their resistance
the blood in our veins is of legends
doctors
poets
musicians
we will not be nameless
they cannot shame us with their propaganda
demand our silence through their genocide
we will not hide behind their trinkets
their choo choo trains
and hockey rinks
we are Detroiters
the Black mecca of possibility
we will not go quietly into the night
we carry the fight of Joe Louis
got the Black fist to prove it
we are warriors and artists
the innovators
they call arsonists in October
they run us over when we resist them
but we're persistent
generations of resilience
we wage love in a world out to get us
productive despite their insistence
Detroit, the city we won't let die
no matter how much
they try us

ESSAYS/ARTICLES

I thought it was important for me to share with the readers of my 2nd poetry book some of the other ways I have expressed myself personally and politically. I also thought it was important to capture this political moment in movement history.

Here you get to go deeper inside my thoughts, as they were, as they may still be.

DETROIT AND THE BLACK WOMAN CONDITION

Historically, Black women have been one of the most marginalized groups in the United States. We are often left to lead, as one of my comrades would say, "a life of quiet desperation." If we are vocal about our conditions, we are "angry Black women." If we are silent about our conditions, we are "lazy Black women." If we utilize the limited resources afforded to us as a result of our conditions, which are symptoms of white supremacist policies resulting in institutionalized racism, then we are "Black women looking for a handout." The Black woman is a punching bag for the dominate culture - governed by capitalism, racism, materialism and militarism.

The water shutoffs in Detroit are a form of violence rooted in racism and sexism. The city is over 80% Black with households led predominately by Black women.

Black women are on the receiving end of tens of thousands of water shutoffs, tens of thousands of tax foreclosures, the commodification of our bodies, and the dehumanization of our image by media, movies, television and the music industry.

Our exposure is compounded by the fact that Detroit as a city has suffered under propaganda assault for over half a century. White flight out of the city, and the subsequent leveling of prosperous Black neighborhoods by racist government officials, provided the corporate owned media an opportunity to manipulate the narrative away from the Black prosperity and self-determination it was witnessing in neighborhoods like Paradise Valley/Black Bottom, and misdirect it towards the labeling of Blacks as perpetrators of most of the blight you see around the city today. The fact that neighborhoods were leveled for expressways is of no consequence to those who like to tell the whitened version of the Detroit comeback story.

Recently, Black residents have complained of having their community gardens "accidentally" leveled by the city, some on multiple occasions, while many young whites are receiving stipends to move into the Detroit and grow gardens, while being hailed in the media as saviors.

Detroit, one of the last major Black meccas in the United States is rapidly being gentrified. The "less desirable" aka Black residents (which means predominately Black women led households) are being expeditiously marginalized and displaced. The water shutoff tragedy is directly connected to this displacement and linked to the tax foreclosure crisis - which too many capitalists are seeing as an opportunity to "buy cheap property," with total disregard for the families being evicted. This is creating antagonistic interactions all over the city, with mothers rushing to remove their belongings and their children, in the face of tax property purchasers, who often lack patience and humanity for the families they are making homeless.

Also, while many in the city are applauding the rapid removal of blight, the fact that foreclosures are 80% responsible for that blight, is information lost on many. To ignore this phenomenon, is to turn a blind eye to the black eye being waged upon Black families - Black mothers and children. Although it cannot be argued that there are indeed structures that need to be removed, we must also struggle against the cause of those blighted out structures.

We cannot be silent while Black mothers are forced to hide their children from being taken away, are unable to bathe their children, or properly nourish their children, because they do not have access to clean, affordable water. We cannot be silent while children are ashamed to go to school because they do not have clean clothing or clean bodies, because their water has been shut off. We cannot be silent while entire communities risk the threat of illness, disease and contamination because families are unable to sanitize their homes or take their medications. We cannot be silent while Black mothers are forced to run from house to house, seeking water to make baby food for their infants. We cannot be silent while homes are being ripped from underneath Black mothers and children by the thousands - blighting entire neighborhoods, making it unsafe for their children to walk to school.

It is no longer an option to say, "That was then, this is now. Racism is in the past." The impact of racist policies and its symptom - internalized oppression must be struggled against. We must become neighbors again. We have a responsibility to not only work to dismantle our rugged individualism which would have us remain silent in the face of such oppression and adversity, but we have a responsibility to struggle against the policies and structures that have divided and seek to conquer us.

Together we will win. Divided we will be spectators and contributors to the genocide of our people.

It is our time to build a new world together. One of sisterhood rooted in the woman's way of knowing, a society that honors and nurtures our humanity and our need for interdependence.

Originally published:
http://www.blackbottomarchives.com/allaboutdetroit/detroit-and-the-black-woman-condition?rq=Tawana%20Petty

{R}EVOLUTION

I've learned from my experience struggling with Grace these past few years, that she appreciates spirited debate rooted in study, love and care and concern for living beings. I have the profound pleasure of being on the board of the James and Grace Lee Boggs Center to Nurture Community Leadership, and to live in close proximity to Grace.

Having those honors bestowed upon me comes with great privilege and great responsibility. How does a 38 year old never married Black mother, born and raised in Detroit, with limited traditional education, i.e. no degrees, relate to and contribute to the legacy of a highly educated, 100 year old widowed Asian American Philosopher who dared to expand the concept of revolution? I've been doing a lot of soul searching to discover this for myself.

I recall about four years ago, the first time I heard Grace ask, "what time is it on the clock of the world?" She told several of us that we must always be thinking about that, we must always be asking that question. To be honest, when I first heard her say it, it went right over my head. Actually, I didn't give the concept much thought at all, and the more she said it, the more frustrated I became with the fact that it didn't resonate with me the way it appeared to resonate with others.

Over the years, my relationship with Grace and the center has helped me evolve. I've had an ever growing and changing evolution of spirit.

What time is it on the clock of the world? What a profound question and directive, contemporaneously. You mean, I actually have to consider all living beings in how I maneuver through the world?

"I don't know what the Next American Revolution will be like, but we might be able to imagine it, if our imagination were rich enough."

This is the quote by Grace that ends the film American Revolutionary: The Evolution of Grace Lee Boggs. I would also argue that this is Grace's most profound challenge to humanity.

How are we defining revolution? If we look at the etymology of the word, in the 14th century, revolution spoke of celestial bodies. The very nature of the word addressed the revolving door of living beings throughout the history of the earth. Revolution was not an individual concept. It wasn't about humans dominating other species, the planet or each other, for survival. It wasn't about a race to the top, or about race at all. In its raw form, revolution was about our interdependence with all living beings, as well as the inevitable extinction of most.

I was fortunate enough to watch a documentary recently about the horseshoe crab and I was fascinated, frightened and enlightened at the same time. The individualism of the human species has managed to pollute the natural habit of a species that has lived over 450 million years. Scientists, for the (evolution) of mankind, have worked diligently to figure out how to package up and bottle the mystery of a living being that refuses to even mate unless it can mate in the very sand it was birthed in. It is so connected to the earth, the foundation of life, that it will not procreate without that foundation. Imagine if we actually learned from the horseshoe crab instead of studying it and dominating it. What a noble concept.

This brings me to my theory on revolution. I am not convinced that humans are meant to carry forward as a species indefinitely. I do however believe that it is our responsibility to dig into our deepest levels of humanity, to "grow our souls," as Grace has encouraged us to do, while we still inhabit this earth.

The horseshoe crab has endured, because it recognizes its place and responsibility to the earth. It does not dominate for its survival, it is interconnected with it. Horseshoe crabs cling on to one another for procreation and preservation. It is rare that humans are able to trick the horseshoe crab into abandoning its responsibility to replenish the earth from which it came. We could learn a lot from the horseshoe crab, but as Grace has challenged, our imaginations must be rich enough.

Humans must stop functioning on this earth as the end all, be all. We are reliant upon one another for our survival, and how we function throughout the world must reflect that. Revolution from an individualistic, "survival of the fittest," mentality will only speed up our demise. It is up to us to figure out how we want the human species to live out its remaining days and to determine how much longer we have to inhabit the earth.

If we do not begin to expand our concept of revolution, nature will make the revolution despite us.

How does a 38 year old never married Black mother, born and raised in Detroit, with limited traditional education, i.e. no degrees, relate to and contribute to the legacy of a highly educated, 100 year old widowed Asian American Philosopher who dared to expand the concept of revolution? She evolves beyond the categories that limit the possibility of revolution.

originally published at:
http://www.blackbottomarchives.com/short-stories/2015/9/14/revolution

THE HETEROPATRIARCHAL ANTI-GENERATIONAL PILE-ON OF THE BLACK LIVES MATTER MOVEMENT

Black Lives Matter, much like the song cry Black Power of the 1960s, has swept through the imaginations of Black people longing to be free from oppression in America.

The liberation motto, which began as a hashtag, and has since developed into an organized movement against structural racism, was founded by three Black women, Alicia Garza, Patrisse Cullors and Opal Tometi. Its origins began in response to the brutal killing of unarmed teenager Trayvon Martin in 2013 and evolved as the police and vigilante killings of unarmed Blacks escalated in the United States. Unfortunately, because Black Lives Matter was founded by Black women, it has been the subject of a proverbial pile-on of elder, macho criticism.

From the constant barrage of Facebook statuses, to Twitter posts, articles, blogs and interviews, many of the strongest criticizers of Black Lives Matter, are older men, too many of them Black. From the refusal to acknowledge Black Lives Matter as a powerful and timely network of organizers, to the failure to acknowledge Alicia, Patrisse and Opal's contribution to the escalation of resistance in this movement moment in history, many elder Black radicals have forgotten who the true target is and aimed their targets at these three women. I call misogyny.

For the past year, since the murder of Mike Brown in Ferguson, I have found myself in hundreds of debates around these non-constructive attacks on these Black women. I am cognizant of the fact that by identifying these as attacks on women, and calling this misogyny, that I open myself up to these attacks as well. However, I felt compelled to speak-out. I am reminded of Ancestor Audre Lorde's quote, "your silence will not protect you."

Many of the men who have chosen to blog, speak-out or post statuses on social media about Black Lives Matter have spent very little time, if any, even attempting to engage the organizers directly. This is problematic, yet typical.

Historically, Black women's visions have been stomped on in the struggle for liberation in this country. Their work has been co-opted, their intellectual property stolen and their voices made invisible behind the banner of Black male leadership. It is unfortunate that these types of assaults continue in the movement today.

Although Black Lives Matter is an official organization with a national chapter and subsequent chapters all across the globe now, many men won't even acknowledge it's significance. This isn't an argument about ideology, it's a refusal to give Black women their just due.

Many Black men are afforded the opportunity to form organizations, collectives, foundations, and moments of struggle under the banner of revolutionary or activist, with little to no analysis or critique from their peers or followers. This too is problematic, yet typical.

I agree that political education needs to be an instrumental part of our movement for liberation. I agree that we sharpen each other when we struggle through ideological differences. I agree that we must hold each other accountable in this work for our collective freedom. However, it is my hope that before more of these "set those girls straight," criticizers post their next blog, stat or interview on Black Lives Matter, that they at least consider becoming part of the solution.

originally published at:
http://www.blackbottomarchives.com/blackpapersocialjustice/the-heteropatriarchal-anti-generational-pile-on-of-the-black-lives-matter-movement

PALESTINE: BLACK SOLIDARITY IN A WORLD OF ANTI-BLACK RACISM

In May of 2015, I traveled to Palestine in a small delegation for ten days. I had read about Palestine, and had even seen videos about the occupation, but I wasn't mentally or emotionally prepared for the impact my trip would have on me. In fact, I am still processing my trip as I type this. I imagine I will be attempting to process my experiences in Palestine for years to come. However, unfortunately, because of the current climate of anti-Black racism in the United States, the extreme militarization and murders of unarmed Blacks by overzealous and racist police and vigilantes, and the use of water as a weapon - through mass shutoffs, towards Black people, I am not afforded an opportunity to place my work on hold awaiting the reconciliation of my emotions.

Shortly after my invitation to speak at the National Students for Justice in Palestine Conference in Boston on the water injustices in Detroit - the connections between the oppression of Palestinians and Black people became much more clear for me. The control of resources such as water, housing and land had strikingly eerie similarities. The militarized brutality that Black people are experiencing in America and the brutality Palestinians are facing from the Israeli military began to have obvious links. See video "Checkpoint" by hip hop activist Jasiri X after his recent trip to Palestine.

Even before my trip to Palestine, I had been participating in Black/Arab solidarity discussions. Recognizing the need to struggle against anti-Black racism, which is inherent in this country, and extremely prevalent towards Blacks in Dearborn/Dearborn Heights, Michigan, a few of my comrades and I felt we needed to do something to build towards liberating ourselves from the hatred imposed upon us. I expressed to them the antagonistic relationship that also exists between Arab business owners and the Black community in Detroit. This frequently toxic relationship has lead to violent confrontations on several occasions. Although the conversations have been challenging for all of us, I commend my Arab comrades for not only engaging me in these conversations, but for being honest about the anti-Black racism they were witnessing in their own families and communities, and for putting themselves on the line in order to struggle against it.

We acknowledged the role of racist propaganda. They also spoke on the privilege that typically accompanies the pursuit of the American dream – meaning – the lifestyle you can be afforded the further you travel away from your darker roots.

We partnered in small conversations at the James and Grace Lee Boggs Center to Nurture Community Leadership. This was important to me because James and Grace Boggs, along with other revolutionaries I have come to learn from and respect, had long struggled against the conflict in Palestine. It has been an honor to continue in that legacy of work.

These conversations were emotional and at times drudged up anger and frustration, but we remained committed with the understanding that Black Lives and Arab humanity depend upon it.

Upon my return from Palestine, my resolve to struggle against anti-Black racism grew. Some of this was due to the blatant racism I experienced personally while in Palestine/Israel, and some was because of the escalation of racism I was witnessing and experiencing in my own country.

One of the ways to continue the conversation and work towards deepening the contradictions that come with Black solidarity when it often doesn't feel reciprocal, was to organize a discussion with other Black activist/organizers who have been engaged in Palestinian solidarity work and were struggling with similar contradictions.

During the 33rd Annual African World Festival, which was also part of the 50th Anniversary of the Charles H. Wright Museum of African American History, I invited Kristian Davis Bailey, Oya Amakisi, Dawud Walid and Darryl Jordan to join me on a panel titled, *Palestine: Black Solidarity in a World of Anti-Black Racism*. The panel was facilitated by Reverend Mayowa Reynolds.

It proved to be a timely and powerful discussion. Kristian, a recent graduate of Stanford University, and a committed Black/Palestinian solidarity activist, was struck by how many "Arab audience members there were, and how many (mostly young) people came up to me afterwards expressing the need and interest to organize against anti-Black racism within Dearborn's Arab communities."

He recognized that the work would be difficult, but the response from the other young activists solidified his resolve to continue the struggle for liberation. Follow Kristian's recent Black Statement of Solidarity with Palestine.

Another one of the telling moments of the event at the museum was the number of people who stayed behind to continue the conversation and seek further understanding of the Palestinian conflict, nearly an hour after the panel discussion had ended. Most even signed an email list to stay included in the conversation. There were also activists from Jewish Voices for Peace present to show their solidarity with the work.

The struggle for liberation for Black people and Palestinians predates my short 38 year old existence, but as a wise elder once told me, "never tell yourself that it won't happen in your lifetime."
I understand now that I must struggle everyday as though the people will be victorious and I must be committed to visioning and building toward a society where all oppressed peoples can be free and self-determinant, in my lifetime.

originally published at:
http://www.blackbottomarchives.com/blackpapersocialjustice/palestine-black-solidarity-in-a-world-of-anti-black-racism

SOCIAL SOLIDARITY ECONOMY FORUM VISITS NORTH AMERICA

From April 7th – 10, 2016, I had the honor of co-coordinating, along with Emily Kawano from RIPESS, NA, and a local Detroit planning team - a convergence of hundreds in Detroit for the North American Social Solidarity Economy Forum. It was the first time the Social Solidarity Economy Forum had been held in North America. Presenters and participants came from Cuba, Quebec, Spain, Jackson, MS, St. Louis, MO, New York and all across the globe. We also had many participants and presenters from Detroit who shared the work that Detroiters are doing locally, as well as their Detroit collaborations across the globe.

We danced together, performed together, and engaged in political struggle. We struggled around politics, new work and new culture, racism, patriarchy, capitalism and more. We participated in a Theater of the Oppressed workshop hosted by Reg Flowers, a yoga workshop with Gwi-seok Hong, performed in a No Talent Necessary Talent Show hosted by Bryce and danced in respect of indigenous land and our Ancestors thanks to Consuela Lopez.

We successfully held a forum with over 400 participants and had only 1 regular sized garbage bag of waste per day. We hope to take that down to zero waste soon. Thanks to Homespun Hustle, many participants either rented, bought or brought their own utensils and dishes, then washed them at a washing station. We composted our food scraps in order to produce new food, thanks to Ty Petrie.

The young people held it down with their own incredible youth track thanks to the organizing of B. Anthony and we held serious discussions on race and decolonizing the solidarity economy with an entire track thanks to William Copeland, Jessica Gordon Nembhard, Elandria Williams and others.

On April 7th, we had 3 amazing tours: From Growing our Economies to Growing Our Souls (Rich Feldman-Boggs Center), Five Miles to Freedom (Jamon Jordan-Historian) and Incite Focus Fab Lab tours (Blair Evans) and hosted a screening of American Revolutionary: The Evolution of Grace Lee Boggs. From April 8th-10th, we held over 65 workshops and activities and four plenaries.

Plenaries included:

- Building the Movement for a Social Solidarity Economy
- De-colonizing the Solidarity Economy
- Achieving Recognition and Support for the Social Solidarity Economy
- SSE from Latin America/Caribbean to North America

Participants brought and exchanged items and held discussions around their newly found treasures with our swap, thanks to Halima Cassells.

Many folks made the NASSE Forum successful, and we still have much work to do. Thank you to everyone who made the forum possible and who will continue to do the work. Thank you to the coordinating committee, local coordinating team, all presenters, volunteers, to Samaritan Center and the Wellness Center, to our sound engineer, maintenance folks, the Digital Stewards for our wireless mesh set-up and to all of our sponsors.

Thank you to Kehben Grier of the Beehive Design Collective for the designing the cover art for the program.

May we all continue to build towards the world we want to live in.

In love and struggle.

originally published:
http://www.blackbottomarchives.com/allaboutdetroit/2016/4/26/social-solidarity-economy-forum-visits-north-america

POLICE BRUTALITY, DETROIT AND THE HISTORY OF ORGANIZED INTERVENTION

Last week I witnessed what happens when police officers are properly trained in de-escalation and when community members respond accordingly. A scene at the corner of my street, which at its height had at least 12 police cars and 20-30 community members, ended with no lives lost. I am cognizant of the fact that decades of organizing, was at least partially responsible for how the officers responded to the incident on my street. I also have the privilege of knowing officers who joined the flawed system of policing with the hopes of making change within it, as well as the idea that they could somehow contribute to the betterment of their communities. Whether I believe that is possible or not, is less important than acknowledging that there are bodies within the system that at least want to make it better. It is, however, my belief that the system is worthy of indictment, and that those who struggle to keep it abusive, lopsided and unaccountable should follow.

When I think of current day community relations with the Detroit Police Department, I think of the Detroit Coalition Against Police Brutality and Peace Zones 4 Life.

"In 1996, the Detroit Coalition Against Police Brutality was founded by Dr. Gloria House, Marge Parsons and myself, partly in response to the killing in 1992 of Malice Green by Detroit police officers Larry Nevers and Walter Budzyn; and based on information presented at a National Conference of Black Lawyers conference in 1996 on racial sentencing disparities where the topic of police brutality against African American men was identified as a potential organizing focus."

These words are a reflection from Ron Scott, penned in his new organizing manual *How to End Police Brutality*, which is available as an e-Book on Amazon.com. This book reflects on a lengthy history of community resistance, including the founding of the coalition and Peace Zones, as well as the establishment of the Detroit Police Commission.

"For 20 years citizen-police interactions improved. With the emergence of Black command and control officers who acted in a more constitutionally-appropriate manner, police mini-stations, certainty of punishment for police brutality, and the establishment of the Detroit Police Commission in 1974, the strongest in the nation, Detroit saw a noticeable decline in incidents. The operating phrase then was not "community policing" - a phrase much-ballyhooed today-but "community control of police."

Ron's book also acknowledges the present and past history of racial tensions, as well as the legacy of Black officers who stood up in the face of police brutality for Black citizens, but were met with violence from white officers.

"The few Black officers in those days saw themselves as protectors for Black people who were brutalized. In fact, The Guardians was an African American police organization founded in the 1950s for specifically that reason. Fights actually erupted between White and Black police officers in response to the brutal treatment of Blacks by White officers."

Ron Scott's analysis in this book is important and provides a *"strategic map for how organizers and community members should move forward as we struggle to resist police brutality."* It is a timely study for young and elder revolutionaries. Ron Scott has made it clear that the coalition is not against the police, but that they are against police brutality. That sentiment is further reiterated in his book. As activists across the globe struggle for alternatives to policing, and work towards building better community relations with existing police systems, they should make this book part of their libraries.

Be sure to visit www.detroitcoalition.org for more information about the Detroit Coalition Against Police Brutality and Peace Zones 4 Life and attend your local Detroit Police Commission meetings and get your voices heard.

originally published at:
http://www.blackbottomarchives.com/allaboutdetroit/police-brutality-detroit-and-the-history-of-organized-intervention

Ancestor Ron Scott died one month after the original publication of this article.

A Century of Badass

Grace,
Detroit rooted revolutionary
philosophically sound
and evolutionary

Grace was wise beyond 100 years
a century of badass

she was a struggle focused theoretician
Grace projected vision

couldn't be bothered with frivolity
or empty conversations

in constant epoch evaluation
contemplating dialectics

Grace synced her clock
aside the world's
and pushed others at her pace
amazing Grace indeed

brilliant
resilient

if you were weak
Grace could feel it

got no time for fears and grieving
an anti-intellectual
genius

Grace shared her marbles freely
and we, the children of Martin and Malcolm
picked them up

Grace was struggle wrapped in love
and sometimes painful conversations

in Maine
in Detroit

a solutionary
clairvoyant in the struggle

Grace was centuries ahead
well read
and not afraid to read you

Grace was seeds for growing souls
a reluctant growth for many

she was the other half of Jimmy
dynamic duo in the struggle

a Chinese American
Living for Change

a tiny frame, with a mighty voice

she nurtured us the way tough lovers do
Grace was a thinker and a doer

she planted her spirit across the globe
so we don't mourn her death today
plus Grace wouldn't have it anyway

Dear Grace Lee Boggs
you are a giant
defiant,
no go along to get along

Thank you Grace for all your strength
and for all you gave the world to contemplate

(Dedicated to Mama Grace on the day of her memorial, October 31, 2015)

Thank you for all your support. If you would like to let the author know how you felt about the book, feel free to contact the author via email: honeycombthepoet@gmail.com. You can also contact the author at honeycombthepoet.com.

Made in the USA
Middletown, DE
04 September 2016